The 30-Minute Plant Based Diet Cookbook

Vegan Recipes are the Best Way to Lose Weight
Faster and Healthy, Easy to Prepare Quick Meals
in 30 Minute

John Becker

Table of Contents

Introduction

A plant-based diet is a diet based primarily on whole plant foods. It is identical to the regular diet we're used to already, except that it leaves out foods that are not exclusively from plants. Hence, a plant-based diet does away with all types of animal-sourced foods, hydrogenated oils, refined sugars, and processed foods. A whole food plant-based diet comprises not just fruits and vegetables; it also consists of unprocessed or barely-processed oils with healthy monounsaturated fats (like extra-virgin olive oil), whole grains, legumes (essentially lentils and beans), seeds and nuts, as well as herbs and spices.

What makes a plant-based meal (or any meal) fun is the manner with which you make them; the seasoning process; and the combination process that contributes to a fantastic flavor and makes every meal unique and enjoyable. There are lots of delicious recipes (all plant-centered), which will prove helpful in when you intend making mouthwatering, healthy plant-based dishes for personal or household consumption. Provided you're eating these plant-based foods regularly, you'll have very problems with fat or diseases that result from bad dietary habits, and there would be no need for excessive calorie tracking.

Plant-based diet recipes are versatile; they range from colorful Salads to Lentil Stews, and Bean Burritos. The recipes also draw influences from around the globe, with Mexican, Chinese, European, Indian cuisines all part of the vast array of plant-based recipes available to choose from. Why You Ought to Reduce Your Intake of Processed and Animal-Based Foods. You have likely heard over and over that processed food has adverse effects on your health. You might have also been told repeatedly to stay away from foods with lots of preservatives; nevertheless, nobody ever offered any genuine or concrete facts about why you ought to avoid these foods and why they are unsafe. Consequently, let us properly dissect it to help you properly comprehend why you ought to stay away from these healthy eating offenders. They have massive habit-forming characteristics. Humans have a predisposition towards being addicted to some specific foods; however, the reality is that the fault is not wholly ours. Every one of the unhealthy treats we relish now and then triggers the dopamine release in our brains. This creates a pleasurable effect in our brain, but the excitement is usually short-lived. The discharged dopamine additionally causes an attachment connection gradually, and this is the reason some people consistently go back to eat certain unhealthy foods even when they know it's unhealthy and unnecessary.

You can get rid of this by taking out that inducement completely. They are sugar-laden and plenteous in glucose-fructose syrup. Animal-based and processed foods are laden with refined sugars and glucose-fructose syrup which has almost no beneficial food nutrient. An ever-increasing number of studies are affirming what several people presumed from the start; that genetically modified foods bring about inflammatory bowel disease, which consequently makes it increasingly difficult for the body to assimilate essential nutrients. The disadvantages that result from your body being unable to assimilate essential nutrients from consumed foods rightly cannot be overemphasized. Processed and animal-based food products contain plenteous amounts of refined carbohydrates. Indeed, your body requires carbohydrates to give it the needed energy to run body capacities. In any case, refining carbs dispenses with the fundamental supplements; in the way that refining entire grains disposes of the whole grain part. What remains, in the wake of refining, is what's considered as empty carbs or empty calories. These can negatively affect the metabolic system in your body by sharply increasing your blood sugar and insulin quantities. They contain lots of synthetic ingredients. At the point when your body is taking in non-natural ingredients, it regards them as foreign substances.

Your body treats them as a health threat. Your body isn't accustomed to identifying synthetic compounds like sucralose or these synthesized sugars. Hence, in defense of your health against this foreign "aggressor," your body does what it's capable of to safeguard your health. It sets off an immune reaction to tackle this "enemy" compound, which indirectly weakens your body's general disease alertness, making you susceptible to illnesses. The concentration and energy expended by your body in ensuring your immune system remain safe could instead be devoted somewhere else. They contain constituent elements that set off an excitable reward sensation in your body. A part of processed and animal-based foods contain compounds like glucose-fructose syrup, monosodium glutamate, and specific food dyes that can trigger some addiction. They rouse your body to receive a benefit in return whenever you consume them. Monosodium glutamate, for example, is added to many store-bought baked foods. This additive slowly conditions your palates to relish the taste. It gets mental just by how your brain interrelates with your taste sensors.

This reward-centric arrangement makes you crave it increasingly, which ends up exposing you to the danger of over consuming calories.

For animal protein, usually, the expression "subpar" is used to allude to plant proteins since they generally have lower levels of essential amino acids as against animal-sourced protein. Nevertheless, what the vast majority don't know is that large amounts of essential amino acids can prove detrimental to your health. Let me break it down further for you.

Asian Delight with Crunchy Dressing

Preparation Time: 20 minutes
Cooking Time: 10 minutes
Servings: 1 bowl
Ingredients:
Salad Dressing:

> ½ teaspoon of powdered ginger or 1 teaspoon of freshly chopped ginger
> 1 tablespoon of honey
> ¼ cup of rice wine vinegar
> 2 tablespoons of soy sauce
> 3 tablespoons of sesame oil
> 3 tablespoons of creamy peanut butter
> ¼ cup of vegetable oil
> 2 tablespoons of toasted sesame seeds

Salad:

> 1 finely shredded carrot
> 1 thinly sliced red bell pepper
> 6 cups of washed and dried spinach
> ¼ thinly sliced red onion
> 1 thinly sliced cucumber
> ½ pound of snap peas
> ½ cup of roasted peanuts
> 1 tablespoon of toasted sesame seeds

Directions:

> In a medium bowl, mix the dressing ingredients and whisk them well. Do not put the sesame seeds in this dressing mixture.
> Put some water in the pot and bring it to a boil. Add the sugar snap peas and cook them for about 5 minutes until they are crisp and tender. Drain and rinse them repeatedly in cold water so that the peas retain their crispy nature.

In a large bowl, add all the other ingredients for the salad. Put the salad dressing on top so that the veggies are well-coated. Add the toasted sesame seeds. Enjoy this salad when you are not in the mood for anything heavy.

Nutrition:
kcal: 378
Carbohydrates: 11 g
Protein: 18 g
Fat: 27 g

Broccoli Salad the Thai Way

Preparation Time: 10 minutes
Cooking Time: 25 minutes
Servings: 1 portion
Ingredients

- 1 tablespoon of tamari
- ¾ cup of mung beans
- 1 lime
- 2 garlic cloves
- 3 tablespoons of cashew butter
- 1 cucumber
- ¼ ounce of fresh mint
- 1 tablespoon of chili-garlic sauce
- 1 head of artisan lettuce
- 3 Thai chilis
- 6 ounces of broccoli florets
- 2 tablespoons of olive oil
- Salt
- Pepper

Directions:

On high heat, add the mung beans to 3 cups of cold water. After they start boiling, reduce the heat to medium. Allow the beans to simmer, but stir them from time to time. The mung beans will be tender within 20 minutes. Drain the excess water and add some salt.

Mince the garlic and cut the lime in half. In a medium bowl, mix the lime juice, minced garlic, tamari, and cashew butter with chili-garlic sauce. Add 3 tablespoons of warm water. Whisk the mixture well.

Slice the cucumber, cut the broccoli into bite-size pieces, and chop the lettuce. Pick the mint leaves as well. Lastly, slice the Thai chilis.

On a non-stick skillet, put 2 tablespoons of olive oil. Turn the heat to medium-high. Once the oil is hot, add the broccoli florets and cook until they are brown. They will be crisp-tender. Add some pepper and salt to the broccoli and add the lime juice and Thai chilis.

In a shallow bowl, spread some cashew sauce. Add some chopped lettuce, mung beans, broccoli, and cucumber. Add mint leaves and mix the Thai chilies. Add some more cashew sauce and enjoy the salad!

Nutrition:
Calories: 203 kcal
Fat: 1.4g
Carbs: 41.6g
Proteins: 4.8g

Sweet Potato, Corn and Jalapeno Bisque

Preparation Time: 10 minutes
Cooking Time: 15 minutes
Servings: 4

Ingredients:

- 4 ears corn
- 1 seeded and chopped jalapeno
- 4 cups vegetable broth
- 1 tablespoon olive oil
- 3 peeled and cubed sweet potatoes
- 1 chopped onion
- ½ tablespoon salt
- ¼ teaspoon black pepper
- 1 minced garlic clove

Directions:

1. In a pan, heat the oil over medium flame and sauté onion and garlic in it and cook for around 3 minutes. Put broth and sweet potatoes in it and bring it to boil. Reduce the flame and cook it for an additional 10 minutes.
2. Remove it from the stove and blend it with a blender. Again, put it on the stove and add corn, jalapeno, salt, and black pepper and serve it.

Nutrition:
Carbohydrates 31g
Protein 6g
Fats 4g
sugar 11g.

Creamy Pea Soup with Olive Pesto

Preparation Time: 20 minutes
Cooking Time: 20 minutes
Servings: 4

Ingredients:

- 1 grated carrot
- 1 rinsed chopped leek
- 1 minced garlic clove
- 2 tablespoons olive oil
- 1 stem fresh thyme leaves
- 15 ounces rinsed and drained peas
- ½ tablespoon salt
- ¼ teaspoon ground black pepper

- 2 ½ cups vegetable broth
- ¼ cup parsley leaves
- 1 ¼ cups pitted green olives
- 1 teaspoon drained capers
- 1 garlic clove

Directions:

1. Take a pan with oil and put it over medium flame and whisk garlic, leek, thyme, and carrot in it. Cook it for around 4 minutes.
2. Add broth, peas, salt, and pepper and increase the heat. When it starts boiling, lower down the heat and cook it with a lid on for around 15 minutes and remove from heat and blend it.
3. For making pesto whisk parsley, olives, capers, and garlic and blend it in a way that it has little chunks. Top the soup with the scoop of olive pesto.

Nutrition:
Carbohydrates 23g
Protein 6g
Fats 15g
sugar 4g
Calories 230.

Spinach Soup with Dill and Basil

Preparation Time: 10 minutes
Cooking Time: 25 minutes
Servings: 8

Ingredients:

1 pound peeled and diced potatoes
1 tablespoon minced garlic
1 teaspoon dry mustard
6 cups vegetable broth
20 ounces chopped frozen spinach
2 cups chopped onion
1 ½ tablespoons salt
½ cup minced dill
1 cup basil
½ teaspoon ground black pepper

Directions:

Whisk onion, garlic, potatoes, broth, mustard, and salt in a pan and cook it over medium flame. When it starts boiling, low down the heat and cover it with the lid and cook for 20 minutes.

Add the remaining ingredients in it and blend it and cook it for few more minutes and serve it.

Nutrition:
Carbohydrates 12g
Protein 13g
Fats 1g
Calories 165.

Coconut Watercress Soup

Preparation Time: 10 minutes
Cooking Time: 20 minutes
Servings: 4

Ingredients:

1 teaspoon coconut oil
1 onion, diced
¾ cup coconut milk

Directions:

Preparing the ingredients.

Melt the coconut oil in a large pot over medium-high heat. Add the onion and cook until soft, about 5 minutes, then add the peas and the water. Bring to a boil, then lower the heat and add the watercress, mint, salt, and pepper.

Cover and simmer for 5 minutes. Stir in the coconut milk, and purée the soup until smooth in a blender or with an immersion blender.

Try this soup with any other fresh, leafy green—anything from spinach to collard greens to arugula to swiss chard.

Nutrition:
Calories: 160 kcal
Fat: 5g
Carbs: 25g
Proteins: 2g

Roasted Red Pepper and Butternut Squash Soup

Preparation Time: 10 minutes
Cooking Time: 45 minutes
Servings: 6

Ingredients:

1 small butternut squash
1 tablespoon olive oil
1 teaspoon sea salt
2 red bell peppers
1 yellow onion
1 head garlic
2 cups water, or vegetable broth
Zest and juice of 1 lime
1 to 2 tablespoons tahini
Pinch cayenne pepper
½ teaspoon ground coriander
½ teaspoon ground cumin
Toasted squash seeds (optional)

Directions:

Preparing the ingredients.

Preheat the oven to 350°f.

Prepare the squash for roasting by cutting it in half lengthwise, scooping out the seeds, and poking some holes in the flesh with a fork. Reserve the seeds if desired.

Rub a small amount of oil over the flesh and skin, then rub with a bit of sea salt and put the halves skin-side down in a large baking dish. Put it in the oven while you prepare the rest of the vegetables.

Prepare the peppers the exact same way, except they do not need to be poked.

Slice the onion in half and rub oil on the exposed faces. Slice the top off the head of garlic and rub oil on the exposed flesh.

After the squash has cooked for 20 minutes, add the peppers, onion, and garlic, and roast for another 20 minutes. Optionally, you can toast the squash seeds by putting them in the oven in a separate baking dish 10 to 15 minutes before the vegetables are finished.

Keep a close eye on them. When the vegetables are cooked, take them out and let them cool before handling them. The squash will be very soft when poked with a fork.

Scoop the flesh out of the squash skin into a large pot (if you have an immersion blender) or into a blender.

Chop the pepper roughly, remove the onion skin and chop the onion roughly, and squeeze the garlic cloves out of the head, all into the pot or blender. Add the water, the lime zest and juice, and the tahini. Purée the soup, adding more water if you like, to your desired consistency. Season with the salt, cayenne, coriander, and cumin. Serve garnished with toasted squash seeds (if using).

Nutrition:
Calories: 156
Protein: 4g
total Fat: 7g
saturated Fat: 11g
carbohydrates: 22g
Fiber: 5g

Cauliflower Spinach Soup

Preparation Time: 30 minutes
Cooking Time: 25 minutes
Servings: 5

Ingredients:

1/2 cup unsweetened coconut milk
5 oz fresh spinach, chopped
5 watercress, chopped
8 cups vegetable stock
1 lb cauliflower, chopped
Salt

Directions:

Add stock and cauliflower in a large saucepan and bring to
boil over medium heat for 15 minutes.

Add spinach and watercress and cook for another 10
minutes.
Remove from heat and puree the soup using a blender until
smooth.
Add coconut milk and stir well. Season with salt.
Stir well and serve hot.

Nutrition:
Calories: 271 kcal
Fat: 3.7g
Carbs: 54g
Proteins: 6.5g

Avocado Mint Soup

Preparation Time: 10 minutes
Cooking Time: 10 minutes
Servings: 2

Ingredients:

1 medium avocado, peeled, pitted, and cut into pieces
1 cup coconut milk
2 romaine lettuce leaves
20 fresh mint leaves
1 tbsp fresh lime juice
1/8 tsp salt

Directions:

Add all ingredients into the blender and blend until
    smooth. Soup should be thick not as a puree.
Pour into the serving bowls and place in the refrigerator for
    10 minutes.
Stir well and serve chilled.

Nutrition:
Calories: 377 kcal
Fat: 14.9g
Carbs: 60.7g
Protein: 6.4g

Creamy Squash Soup

Preparation Time: 10 minutes
Cooking Time: 25 minutes
Servings: 8

Ingredients:

3 cups butternut squash, chopped
1 ½ cups unsweetened coconut milk
1 tbsp coconut oil
1 tsp dried onion flakes
1 tbsp curry powder
4 cups water
1 garlic clove
1 tsp kosher salt

Directions:

Add squash, coconut oil, onion flakes, curry powder, water, garlic, and salt into a large saucepan. Bring to boil over high heat.

Turn heat to medium and simmer for 20 minutes.

Puree the soup using a blender until smooth. Return soup to the saucepan and stir in coconut milk and cook for 2 minutes.
Stir well and serve hot.

Nutrition:
Calories: 271 kcal
Fat: 3.7g
Carbs: 54g
Protein:6.5g

Zucchini Soup

Preparation Time: 10 minutes
Cooking Time: 15 minutes
Servings: 8

Ingredients:

2 ½ lbs zucchini, peeled and sliced
1/3 cup basil leaves
4 cups vegetable stock
4 garlic cloves, chopped
2 tbsp olive oil
1 medium onion, diced
Pepper
Salt

Directions:

Heat olive oil in a pan over medium-low heat.

Add zucchini and onion and sauté until softened. Add garlic and sauté for a minute.

Add vegetable stock and simmer for 15 minutes.

Remove from heat. Stir in basil and puree the soup using a blender until smooth and creamy. Season with pepper and salt.

Stir well and serve.

Nutrition:
Calories: 434 kcal
Fat: 35g
Carbs: 27g
Protein: 6.7g

Creamy Celery Soup

Preparation Time: 20 minutes
Cooking Time: 20 minutes
Servings: 4

Ingredients:

6 cups celery
½ tsp dill
2 cups water
1 cup coconut milk
1 onion, chopped
Pinch of salt

Directions:

Add all ingredients into the electric pot and stir well.
Cover electric pot with the lid and select soup setting.
Release pressure using a quick release method than open
the lid.

Puree the soup using an immersion blender until smooth
and creamy.
Stir well and serve warm.

Nutrition:
Calories: 159kcal
Fat: 8.4g
Carbs: 19.8g
Proteins: 4.6g

Avocado Cucumber Soup

Preparation Time: 20 minutes
Cooking Time: 0 minutes
Servings: 3

Ingredients:

1 large cucumber, peeled and sliced
¾ cup water
¼ cup lemon juice
2 garlic cloves
6 green onion
2 avocados, pitted
½ tsp black pepper
½ tsp pink salt

Directions:

Add all ingredients into the blender and blend until smooth and creamy.
Place in refrigerator for 30 minutes.
Stir well and serve chilled.

Nutrition:

Calories: 127 kcal
Fat: 6.6g
Carbs: 13g
Protein: 0.7g

Garden Vegetable Stew

Preparation Time: 5 minutes
Cooking Time: 60 minutes
Servings: 4

Ingredients:

- 2 tablespoons olive oil
- 1 medium red onion, chopped
- 1 medium carrot, cut into 1/4-inch slices
- 1/2 cup dry white wine
- 3 medium new potatoes, unpeeled and cut into 1-inch pieces
- 1 medium red bell pepper, cut into 1/2-inch dice
- 11/2 cups vegetable broth
- 1 tablespoon minced fresh savory or 1 teaspoon dried

Directions:

In a large saucepan, heat the oil over medium heat. Add the onion and carrot, cover, and cook until softened, 7 minutes. Add the wine and cook, uncovered, for 5 minutes. Stir in the potatoes, bell pepper, and broth and bring to a boil. Reduce the heat to medium and simmer for 15 minutes.

Add the zucchini, yellow squash, and tomatoes. Season with salt and black pepper to taste, cover, and simmer until the vegetables are tender, 20 to 30 minutes. Stir in the corn, peas, basil, parsley, and savory. Taste, adjusting seasonings if necessary. Simmer to blend flavors, about 10 minutes more. Serve immediately.

Nutrition:

Calories: 219 kcal
Fat: 4.5g
Carbs: 38.2g
Protein: 6.4g

Moroccan Vermicelli Vegetable Soup

Preparation Time: 5 minutes
Cooking Time: 35 minutes
Servings: 4 to 6

Ingredients:

1 tablespoon olive oil
1 small onion, chopped
1 large carrot, chopped
1 celery rib, chopped
3 small zucchini, cut into 1/4-inch dice
1 (28-ounce) can diced tomatoes, drained
2 tablespoons tomato paste
11/2 cups cooked or 1 (15.5-ounce) can chickpeas, drained
    and rinsed
2 teaspoons smoked paprika
1 teaspoon ground cumin
1 teaspoon za'atar spice (optional)
1/4 teaspoon ground cayenne
6 cups vegetable broth, homemade (see light vegetable
    broth) or store-bought, or water

Salt

4 ounces vermicelli

2 tablespoons minced fresh cilantro, for garnish

Directions:

In a large soup pot, heat the oil over medium heat. Add the onion, carrot, and celery. Cover and cook until softened, about 5 minutes. Stir in the zucchini, tomatoes, tomato paste, chickpeas, paprika, cumin, za'atar, and cayenne.

Add the broth and salt to taste. Bring to a boil, then reduce heat to low and simmer, uncovered, until the vegetables are tender, about 30 minutes.

Shortly before serving, stir in the vermicelli and cook until the noodles are tender, about 5 minutes. Ladle the soup into bowls, garnish with cilantro, and serve.

Nutrition:

Calories: 236 kcal

Fat: 1.8g

Carbs: 48.3g

Protein: 7g

Moroccan Vegetable Stew

Preparation Time: 5 minutes
Cooking Time: 35 minutes
Servings: 4

Ingredients:

- 1 tablespoon olive oil
- 2 medium yellow onions, chopped
- 2 medium carrots, cut into 1/2-inch dice
- 1/2 teaspoon ground cumin
- 1/2 teaspoon ground cinnamon or allspice
- 1/2 teaspoon ground ginger
- 1/2 teaspoon sweet or smoked paprika
- 1/2 teaspoon saffron or turmeric

- 1 (14.5-ounce) can diced tomatoes, undrained
- 8 ounces green beans, trimmed and cut into 1-inch pieces
- 2 cups peeled, seeded, and diced winter squash
- 1 large russet or other baking potato, peeled and cut into 1/2-inch dice
- 11/2 cups vegetable broth
- 11/2 cups cooked or 1 (15.5-ounce) can chickpeas, drained and rinsed
- ¾ cup frozen peas
- 1/2 cup pitted dried plums (prunes)
- 1 teaspoon lemon zest
- Salt and freshly ground black pepper
- 1/2 cup pitted green olives
- 1 tablespoon minced fresh cilantro or parsley, for garnish
- 1/2 cup toasted slivered almonds, for garnish

Directions:

1. In a large saucepan, heat the oil over medium heat. Add the onions and carrots, cover, and cook for 5 minutes. Stir in the cumin, cinnamon, ginger, paprika, and saffron. Cook, uncovered, stirring, for 30 seconds.

2. Add the tomatoes, green beans, squash, potato, and broth and bring to a boil. Reduce heat to low, cover, and simmer until the vegetables are tender, about 20 minutes.

3. Add the chickpeas, peas, dried plums, and lemon zest. Season with salt and pepper to taste. Stir in the olives and simmer, uncovered, until the flavors are blended, about 10 minutes. Sprinkle with cilantro and almonds and serve immediately.

Nutrition:
Calories: 71 kcal
Fat: 2.8g
Carbs: 9.8g
Protein: 3.7g

Basic Recipe for Vegetable Broth

Preparation Time: 10 Minutes
Cooking Time: 60 Minutes
Servings: Makes 2 Quarts
Ingredients:

8 cups Water
1 Onion, chopped
4 Garlic cloves, crushed
2 Celery Stalks, chopped
Pinch of Salt
1 Carrot, chopped
Dash of Pepper
1 Potato, medium & chopped
1 tbsp. Soy Sauce
3 Bay Leaves

Directions:

To make the vegetable broth, you need to place all of the
ingredients in a deep saucepan.

Heat the pan over a medium-high heat. Bring the vegetable
mixture to a boil.

Once it starts boiling, lower the heat to medium-low and
allow it to simmer for at least an hour or so. Cover it
with a lid.

When the time is up, pass it through a filter and strain the
vegetables, garlic, and bay leaves.

Allow the stock to cool completely and store in an air-tight
container.

Nutrition:
Calories: 44 kcal
Fat: 0.6g
Carbs: 9.7g
Protein: 0.9g

Cucumber Dill Gazpacho

Preparation Time: 10 Minutes
Cooking Time: 2 hours
Serving Size: 4
Ingredients:

4 large cucumbers, peeled, deseeded, and chopped
1/8 tsp salt
1 tsp chopped fresh dill + more for garnishing
2 tbsp freshly squeezed lemon juice
1 ½ cups green grape, seeds removed
3 tbsp extra virgin olive oil
1 garlic clove, minced

Directions:

Add all the ingredients to a food processor and blend until
   smooth.
Pour the soup into serving bowls and chill for 1 to 2 hours.
Garnish with dill and serve chilled.

Nutrition:

Calories: 236 kcal
Fat: 1.8g
Carbs: 48.3g
Protein: 7g

Red Lentil Soup

Preparation Time: 5 Minutes
Cooking Time: 25 Minutes
Servings: Makes 6 cups
Ingredients:

 2 tbsp. Nutritional Yeast
 1 cup Red Lentil, washed
 ½ tbsp. Garlic, minced
 4 cups Vegetable Stock
 1 tsp. Salt
 2 cups Kale, shredded
 3 cups Mixed Vegetables

Directions:

To start with, place all ingredients needed to make the soup in a large pot.

Heat the pot over medium-high heat and bring the mixture to a boil.

Once it starts boiling, lower the heat to low. Allow the soup to simmer.

Simmer it for 10 to 15 minutes or until cooked. Serve and enjoy.

Nutrition:
Calories: 212 kcal
Fat: 11.9g
Carbs: 31.7g
Protein: 7.3g

Coconut and Grilled Vegetable Soup

Preparation Time: 10 Minutes
Cooking Time: 45 Minutes
Servings: 4
Ingredients:

- 2 small red onions cut into wedges
- 2 garlic cloves
- 10 oz. butternut squash, peeled and chopped
- 10 oz. pumpkins, peeled and chopped
- 4 tbsp melted vegan butter
- Salt and black pepper to taste
- 1 cup of water
- 1 cup unsweetened coconut milk
- 1 lime juiced
- ¾ cup vegan mayonnaise
- Toasted pumpkin seeds for garnishing

Directions:

Preheat the oven to 400 F.

On a baking sheet, spread the onions, garlic, butternut squash, and pumpkins and drizzle half of the butter on top. Season with salt, black pepper, and rub the seasoning well onto the vegetables. Roast in the oven for 45 minutes or until the vegetables are golden brown and softened.

Transfer the vegetables to a pot; add the remaining ingredients except for the pumpkin seeds and using an immersion blender puree the ingredients until smooth.

Dish the soup, garnish with the pumpkin seeds and serve warm.

Nutrition:

Calories 290
Fat 10 g
Protein 30 g
Carbohydrates 0 g

Tofu Goulash Soup

Preparation Time: 35 Minutes
Cooking Time: 20 Minutes
Servings: 4

Ingredients:

4¼ oz. vegan butter
1 white onion, chopped
2 garlic cloves, minced
1 ½ cups butternut squash
1 red bell pepper, deseeded and chopped
1 tbsp paprika powder
¼ tsp red chili flakes
1 tbsp dried basil
½ tbsp crushed cardamom seeds
Salt and black pepper to taste
1 ½ cups crushed tomatoes
3 cups vegetable broth
1½ tsp red wine vinegar
Chopped parsley to serve

Directions:

Place the tofu between two paper towels and allow draining of water for 30 minutes. After, crumble the tofu and set aside.

Melt the vegan butter in a large pot over medium heat and sauté the onion and garlic until the veggies are fragrant and soft, 3 minutes.

Stir in the tofu and cook until golden brown, 3 minutes.

Add the butternut squash, bell pepper, paprika, red chili flakes, basil, cardamom seeds, salt, and black pepper. Cook for 2 minutes to release some flavor and mix in the tomatoes and 2 cups of vegetable broth.

Close the lid, bring the soup to a boil, and then simmer for 10 minutes.

Stir in the remaining vegetable broth, the red wine vinegar, and adjust the taste with salt and black pepper.

Dish the soup, garnish with the parsley and serve warm.

Nutrition:
Calories 320
Fat 10 g
Protein 10 g
Carbohydrates 20 g

Pesto Pea Soup

Preparation Time: 10 Minutes
Cooking Time: 20 Minutes
Servings: 4
Ingredients:

    2 cups Water
    8 oz. Tortellini
    ¼ cup Pesto
    1 Onion, small & finely chopped
    1 lb. Peas, frozen
    1 Carrot, medium & finely chopped
    1 ¾ cup Vegetable Broth, less sodium
    1 Celery Rib, medium & finely chopped

Directions:

To start with, boil the water in a large pot over a medium-high heat.

Next, stir in the tortellini to the pot and cook it following the instructions given in the packet.

In the meantime, cook the onion, celery, and carrot in a deep saucepan along with the water and broth.

Cook the celery-onion mixture for 6 minutes or until softened.

Now, spoon in the peas and allow it to simmer while keeping it uncovered.

Cook the peas for few minutes or until they are bright green and soft.

Then, spoon in the pesto to the peas mixture. Combine well.

Pour the mixture into a high-speed blender and blend for 2 to 3 minutes or until you get a rich, smooth soup.

Return the soup to the pan. Spoon in the cooked tortellini.

Finally, pour into a serving bowl and top with more cooked peas if desired.

Tip: If desired, you can season it with Maldon salt at the end.

Nutrition:

Calories 100

Fat 0 g

Protein 0 g

Carbohydrates 0 g

Tofu and Mushroom Soup

Preparation Time: 15 Minutes
Cooking Time: 10 Minutes
Servings: 4

Ingredients:

2 tbsp olive oil
1 garlic clove, minced
1 large yellow onion, finely chopped
1 tsp freshly grated ginger
1 cup vegetable stock
2 small potatoes, peeled and chopped
¼ tsp salt
¼ tsp black pepper
2 (14 oz) silken tofu, drained and rinsed
2/3 cup baby Bella mushrooms, sliced
1 tbsp chopped fresh oregano
2 tbsp chopped fresh parsley to garnish

Directions:

Heat the olive oil in a medium pot over medium heat and sauté the garlic, onion, and ginger until soft and fragrant.

Pour in the vegetable stock, potatoes, salt, and black pepper. Cook until the potatoes soften, 12 minutes.

Stir in the tofu and using an immersion blender, puree the ingredients until smooth.

Mix in the mushrooms and simmer with the pot covered until the mushrooms warm up while occasionally stirring to ensure that the tofu doesn't curdle, 7 minutes.

Stir oregano, and dish the soup.

Garnish with the parsley and serve warm.

Nutrition:

Calories 310

Fat 10 g

Protein 40.0 g

Carbohydrates 0 g

Avocado Green Soup

Preparation Time: 5 Minutes
Cooking Time: 5 Minutes
Servings: 4

Ingredients:

2 tbsp olive oil
1 ½ cup fresh kale, chopped coarsely
1 ½ cup fresh spinach, chopped coarsely
3 large avocados, halved, pitted and pulp extracted
2 cups of soy milk
2 cups no-sodium vegetable broth
3 tbsp chopped fresh mint leaves
¼ tsp salt
¼ tsp black pepper
2 limes, juiced

Directions:

Heat the olive oil in a medium saucepan over medium heat
and mix in the kale and spinach. Cook until wilted, 3
minutes and turn off the heat.
Add the remaining ingredients and using an immersion
blender, puree the soup until smooth.
Dish the soup and serve immediately.

Nutrition:
Calories 400
Fat 10 g
Protein 20 g
Carbohydrates 30 g

Black Bean Nacho Soup

Preparation Time: 5 Minutes
Cooking Time: 30 Minutes
Servings: 4
Ingredients:

30 oz. Black Bean
1 tbsp. Olive Oil
2 cups Vegetable Stock
½ of 1 Onion, large & chopped
2 ½ cups Water
3 Garlic cloves, minced
14 oz. Mild Green Chillies, diced
1 tsp. Cumin
1 cup Salsa
½ tsp. Salt
16 oz. Tomato Paste

½ tsp. Black Pepper

Directions:

For making this delicious fare, heat oil in a large pot over medium-high heat.

Once the oil becomes hot, stir in onion and garlic to it.

Sauté for 4 minutes or until the onion is softened.

Next, spoon in chilli powder, salt, cumin, and pepper to the pot. Mix well.

Then, stir in tomato paste, salsa, water, green chillies, and vegetable stock to onion mixture. Combine.

Bing the mixture to a boil. Allow the veggies to simmer.

When the mixture starts simmering, add the beans.

Bring the veggie mixture to a simmer again and lower the heat to low.

Finally, cook for 15 to 20 minutes and check for seasoning. Add more salt and pepper if needed.

Garnish with the topping of your choice. Serve it hot.

Nutrition:

Calories 270

Fat 10 g

Protein 10 g

Carbohydrates 10 g

Potato Leek Soup

Preparation Time: 5 Minutes
Cooking Time: 5 Minutes
Servings: 4
Ingredients:

- 1 cup fresh cilantro leaves
- 6 garlic cloves, peeled
- 3 tbsp vegetable oil
- 3 leeks, white and green parts chopped
- 2 lb russet potatoes, peeled and chopped
- 1 tsp cumin powder
- ¼ tsp salt
- ¼ tsp black pepper
- 2 bay leaves
- 6 cups no-sodium vegetable broth

Directions:

In a spice blender, process the cilantro and garlic until
smooth paste forms.

Heat the vegetable oil in a large pot and sauté the garlic
    mixture and leeks until the leeks are tender, 5 minutes.
Mix in the remaining ingredients and allow boiling until the
    potatoes soften, 15 minutes.
Turn the heat off, open the lid, remove and discard the bay
    leaves.
Using an immersion blender, puree the soup until smooth.
Dish the food and serve warm.

Nutrition:
Calories 215
Fat 0 g
Protein 10 g
Carbohydrates 20.0 g

Lentil Soup

Preparation Time: 15 Minutes
Cooking Time: 25 Minutes
Servings: 4
Ingredients:

  1 tbsp. Olive Oil
  4 cups Vegetable Stock
  1 Onion, finely chopped
  2 Carrots, medium
  1 cup Lentils, dried
  1 tsp. Cumin

Directions:

To make this healthy soup, first, you need to heat the oil in
   a medium-sized skillet over medium heat.
Once the oil becomes hot, stir in the cumin and then the
   onions.

Sauté them for 3 minutes or until the onion is slightly transparent and cooked.

To this, add the carrots and toss them well.

Next, stir in the lentils. Mix well.

Now, pour in the vegetable stock and give a good stir until everything comes together.

As the soup mixture starts to boil, reduce the heat and allow it to simmer for 10 minutes while keeping the pan covered.

Turn off the heat and then transfer the mixture to a bowl.

Finally, blend it with an immersion blender or in a high-speed blender for 1 minute or until you get a rich, smooth mixture.

Serve it hot and enjoy.

Nutrition:

Calories: 266

Fat: 13

Fiber: 8

Carbs: 10

Protein: 11

Kale White Bean Soup

Preparation Time: 10 Minutes
Cooking Time: 45 Minutes
Servings: 4
Ingredients:

  1 Onion, medium & finely sliced
  3 cups Kale, coarsely chopped
  2 tsp. Olive Oil
  15 oz. White Beans
  4 cups Vegetable Broth
  4 Garlic Cloves, minced
  Sea Salt & Pepper, as needed
  2 tsp. Rosemary, fresh & chopped
  1 lb. White Potatoes, cubed

Directions:

Begin by taking a large saucepan and heat it over a
medium-high heat.

Once the pan becomes hot, spoon in the oil.

Next, stir in the onion and sauté for 8 to 9 minutes or until
the onions are cooked and lightly browned.

Then, add the garlic and rosemary to the pan.

Sauté for a further minute or until aromatic.

Now, pour in the broth along with the potatoes, black
pepper, and salt. Mix well.

Bring the mixture to a boil, and when it starts boiling, lower
the heat.

Allow it to simmer for 32 to 35 minutes or until the potatoes
are cooked and tender.

After that, mash the potatoes slightly by using the back of
the spoon.

Finally, add the kale and beans to the soup and cook for 8
minutes or until the kale is wilted.

Check the seasoning. Add more salt and pepper if needed.

Serve hot.

Nutrition:
Calories: 198
Fat: 11
Fiber: 1
Carbs: 12
Protein: 12

Black Bean Mushroom Soup

Preparation Time: 10 Minutes
Cooking Time: 40 Minutes
Servings: 2
Ingredients:

    2 tbsp. Olive Oil
    1 clove of Garlic, peeled & minced
    ½ cup Vegetable Stock
    1 tsp. Thyme, dried
    15 oz. Black Beans
    1 2/3 cup Water, hot

oz. Mushrooms
1 Onion, finely chopped
4 Sourdough Bread Slices
Vegan Butter, to serve

Directions:

To begin with, spoon the oil into a medium-sized deep saucepan over a medium heat.

Once the oil becomes hot, stir in the onion and garlic.

Sauté for 5 minutes or until the onion is translucent.

Next, spoon in the mushrooms and thyme. Mix well.

Cook for another 5 minutes or until dark brown.

Then, pour the water into the mixture along with the stock and beans.

Allow it to simmer for 20 minutes or until the mushroom is soft.

Pour the mixture to a high-speed blender and pulse for 1 to 2 minutes until it is smooth yet grainy.

Serve and enjoy.

Nutrition:

Calories: 400
Fat: 32
Fiber: 6
Carbs: 4
Protein: 25

Broccoli Soup

Preparation Time: 5 Minutes
Cooking Time: 15 Minutes
Servings: 2
Ingredients:

    3 cup Vegetable Broth
    2 Green Chili
    2 cups Broccoli Florets
    1 tbsp. Chia Seeds
    1 cup Spinach
    1 tsp. Oil
    4 Celery Stalk
    1 Potato, medium & cubed
    4 Garlic cloves
    Salt, as needed
    Juice of ½ of 1 Lemon

Directions:

First, heat the oil in a large sauté pan over a medium-high heat.

Once the oil becomes hot, add the potatoes to it.

When the potatoes become soft, stir all the remaining ingredients into the pan, excluding the spinach, chia seeds, and lemon.

Cook until the broccoli is soft, and then add the spinach and chia seed to the pan.

Turn off the heat after cooking for 2 minutes.

Allow the spinach mixture to cool slightly. Pour the mixture into a high-speed blender and blend for two minutes or until smooth.

Pour the lemon juice over the soup. Stir and serve immediately.

Enjoy.

Nutrition:

Calories: 200

Fat: 3

Fiber: 2

Carbs: 5

Protein: 4

Squash Lentil Soup

Preparation Time: 10 Minutes
Cooking Time: 35 Minutes
Servings: 4
Ingredients:

   7 cups Vegetable Broth
   2 tbsp. Olive Oil
   2 tsp, Sage dried
   1 Yellow Onion, medium & diced.
   Salt & Pepper to taste
   1 Butternut Squash
   1 ½ cup Red Lentils

Directions:

Start by heating the oil in a large saucepan, and stir in the
      onions.
Sauté the onions for to 2 to 3 minutes or until softened.
Once cooked, stir in squash and sage while stirring
      continuously.
Then, spoon in the lentils, salt, and pepper.

Bring the lentil mixture to a boil for about 30 minutes.
Lower the heat.
Then, allow the soup to cool down until the lentils are soft.
Finally, transfer the mixture to a high-speed blender and
blend for 3 to 4 minutes or until smooth.
Serve hot.

Nutrition:
Calories: 200
Fat: 7
Fiber: 4
Carbs: 7
Protein: 5

Mexican Soup

Preparation Time: 10 Minutes
Cooking Time: 45 Minutes
Servings: 6
Ingredients:

- 2 tbsp. Extra Virgin Olive Oil
- 8 oz. can of Diced Tomatoes & Chilies
- 1 Yellow Onion, diced
- 2 cups Green Lentils
- ½ tsp. Salt
- 2 Celery Stalks, diced
- 8 cups Vegetable Broth
- 2 Carrots, peeled & diced
- 2 cups Diced Tomatoes & Juices
- 3 Garlic cloves, minced

1 Red Bell Pepper, diced
1 tsp. Oregano
1 tbsp. Cumin
¼ tsp. Smoked Paprika
1 Avocado, pitted & diced

Directions:

Heat oil in a large-sized pot over a medium heat.

Once the oil becomes hot, stir in the onion, bell pepper, carrot, and celery into the pot.

Cook the onion mixture for 5 minutes or until the veggies are soft.

Then, spoon in garlic, oregano, cumin, and paprika into it and sauté for one minute or until aromatic.

Next, add the tomatoes, salt, chilies, broth, and lentils to the mixture.

Now, bring the tomato-chili mixture to a boil and allow it to simmer for 32 to 40 minutes or until the lentils become soft.

Check the seasoning and add more if needed.

Serve along with avocado and hot sauce.

Nutrition:

Calories: 344
Fat: 23
Fiber: 12
Carbs: 3
Protein: 16

Medley of Mushroom Soup

Preparation Time: 10 Minutes
Cooking Time: 20 Minutes
Servings: 4
Ingredients:

    4 oz. unsalted vegan butter
    1 small onion, finely chopped
    1 garlic clove, minced
    2 cups sliced mixed mushrooms
    ½ lb celery root, chopped
    ½ tsp dried rosemary
    3 cups of water
    1 vegan stock cube, crushed
    1 tbsp plain vinegar
    1 cup coconut cream
    6 leaves basil, chopped

Directions:

Melt the vegan butter in a medium pot and sauté the onion, garlic, mushrooms, celery, and rosemary until the vegetables soften, 5 minutes.

Stir in the water, stock cube, and vinegar. Cover the pot, allow boiling, and then, simmer for 10 minutes.

Mix in the coconut cream and puree the ingredients using an immersion blender until smooth. Simmer for 2 minutes.

Dish the soup and serve warm.

Nutrition:
Calories: 140
Fat: 3
Fiber: 2
Carbs: 1. 5
Protein: 7

Celery Dill Soup

Preparation Time: 5 Minutes
Cooking Time: 25 Minutes
Servings: 4
Ingredients:

- 2 tbsp. coconut oil
- ½ lb. celery root, trimmed
- 1 garlic clove
- 1 medium white onion
- ¼ cup fresh dill, roughly chopped
- 1 tsp. cumin powder
- ¼ tsp. nutmeg powder
- 1 small head cauliflower, cut into florets
- 3½ cups seasoned vegetable stock
- 5 oz. vegan butter
- Juice from 1 lemon
- ¼ cup coconut cream
- Salt and black pepper to taste

Directions:

1. Melt the coconut oil in a large pot and sauté the celery root, garlic, and onion until softened and fragrant, 5 minutes.

2. Stir in the dill, cumin, and nutmeg, and stir-fry for 1 minute. Mix in the cauliflower and vegetable stock. Allow the soup to boil for 15 minutes and turn the heat off.

3. Add the vegan butter and lemon juice, and puree the soup using an immersion blender.

4. Stir in the coconut cream, salt, black pepper, and dish the soup.

5. Serve warm.

Nutrition:
Calories: 320
Fat: 10g
Protein: 20g
Carbs: 9g

Broccoli Fennel Soup

Preparation Time: 15 Minutes
Cooking Time: 10 Minutes
Servings: 4
Ingredients:

- 1 fennel bulb, white and green parts coarsely chopped
- 10 oz. broccoli, cut into florets
- 3 cups vegetable stock
- Salt and freshly ground black pepper
- 1 garlic clove
- 1 cup dairy-free cream cheese
- 3 oz. vegan butter
- ½ cup chopped fresh oregano

Directions:

1. In a medium pot, combine the fennel, broccoli, vegetable stock, salt, and black pepper. Bring to a boil until the vegetables soften, 10 to 15 minutes.

2. Stir in the remaining ingredients and simmer the soup for 3 to 5 minutes.

3. Adjust the taste with salt and black pepper, and dish the soup.

4. Serve warm.

Nutrition:
Calories: 240
Fat: 8g
Protein: 5g
Carbs: 12g

Curry Recipes

Coconut Tofu Curry

Preparation Time: 30 Minutes
Cooking Time: 15 Minutes
Serving: 2
Ingredients:

- 1 14-oz. block firm tofu

- 2 teaspoon coconut oil

- 1 medium sweet onion, diced

- 1 13-oz. can reduced-Fat coconut milk

- 1 cup fresh tomatoes, diced

- 1 cup snap peas

- 1 1/2 inch ginger, finely minced

- 1 teaspoon curry powder

- 1 teaspoon turmeric

- 1 teaspoon cumin

- 1/2 teaspoon red pepper flakes

- 1 teaspoon agave nectar

- 1/4 teaspoon Salt

- 1/4 teaspoon pepper to taste

Directions:

1. Cut the tofu into 1/2-inch cubes.

2. Heat the coconut oil in a large skillet over medium-high heat.

3. Add the tofu and cook for about 5 minutes.

4. Stir in the garlic and diced onions, and sauté until the onions are transparent (for about 5 to 10 minutes); add the ginger while stirring.

5. Add in the coconut milk, tomatoes, agave nectar, snap peas, and remaining spices.

6. Combine thoroughly, cover, and cook on low heat; remove after 10 minutes of cooking.

7. For serving, scoop the curry into a bowl or over rice.

Nutrition:
Calories 751
Total Fat 58g
Cholesterol 0mg
Sodium 356mg
Total Carbohydrate 44.8g

Green Thai Curry

Preparation Time: 30 Minutes
Cooking Time: 18 Minutes
Serving: 4
Ingredients:

- 1 cup white rice

- 1/2 cup dry chickpeas

- 2 tablespoon olive oil

- 1 14-oz. package firm tofu, drained

- 1 medium green bell pepper

- 1/2 white onion, diced

- 2 tablespoon green curry paste

- 1 cup reduced-Fat coconut milk

- 1 cup water

- 1 cup peas, fresh or frozen

- 1/3 cup chopped fresh Thai basil

- 2 tablespoon maple syrup

- 1/2 teaspoon lime juice

- 1/4 teaspoon salt

Directions:

1. Cut the tofu into 1/2-inch pieces.

2. Over medium-high heat, heat up the olive oil in a large skillet and fry the tofu about 3 minutes per side.

3. Remove the skillet from the stove and set the tofu aside in a medium-sized bowl with the cooked chickpeas.

4. Using the same skillet over medium-high heat, add the bell pepper and onions and sauté until they are softened, for about 5 minutes.

5. Remove the skillet from the heat, add the green curry paste, water (or vegetable broth), and coconut milk to the skillet.

6. Stir until the curry paste is well incorporated; then add the tofu, chickpeas, and peas to the mixture and cook for 10 more minutes.

7. Drop in the Thai basil, maple syrup, and salt, and bring the mixture back up to a low cooking bubble, stirring constantly for about 3 minutes. Remove from heat.

8. Serve with rice, topped with additional chopped Thai basil, or store for later!

Nutrition: Calories 621,Total Fat 29g,Saturated Fat 14.8g Cholesterol 0mg,Sodium 482mg,Total Carbohydrate 75.2g

Coconut Curry with Cauliflower and Tomato

Preparation Time: 10 Minutes
Cooking Time: 30 Minutes
Serving: 6
Ingredients:

- 3 cups Cooked brown rice for serving

- 2 tablespoons olive oil

- 1 onion, chopped

- 1 pound sweet potato, unpeeled but chopped

- 1 head cauliflower, chopped

- 1 teaspoon kosher salt, divided

- 1 tablespoon garam masala

- 1 teaspoon cumin

- 1/4 teaspoon cayenne pepper

- 2 tablespoons curry powder

- 1 23-ounce jar diced plum tomatoes

- 1 15-ounce can full-Fat coconut milk

- 15-ounce can chickpeas, rinsed and drained

- 4 cups fresh spinach leaves

- 1 tablespoon Cilantro for garnish

Directions:

1. Heat the oil in a large pot over medium heat.

2. Sauté the onions for about three minutes, then add the sweet potato and sauté for another 3 minutes.

3. Add the cauliflower and a half teaspoon of the salt; sauté for five minutes.

4. Add the garam marsala, cumin, cayenne pepper and curry powder; stir to mix thoroughly.

5. Pour in the plum tomatoes, including their juice and the coconut milk; bring to a boil.

6. Reduce the heat and simmer, covered, for about 10 minutes. The cauliflower should be soft.

7. Add the chickpeas and spinach leaves, along with the rest of the salt; stir until the spinach wilts and the chickpeas are heated through.

8. Serve over brown rice and garnish with cilantro.

Nutrition:
Calories 1042
Total Fat 39.9g
Saturated Fat 29.2g
Cholesterol 0mg
Sodium 508mg
Total Carbohydrate 145.2g

Satay Sweet Potato Curry

Preparation Time: 6 Minutes
Cooking Time: 10 Minutes
Serving: 8
Ingredients:

- 2 tablespoons coconut oil

- 4 cloves garlic, grated

- 6 tablespoons Thai red curry paste

- 2 pounds sweet potato, peeled, cubed

- 14 ounces spinach

- 2 onions, chopped

- 3 tablespoons minced ginger

- 2 tablespoons smooth peanut butter

- 14 ounces coconut milk

- Juice, 2 limes

- Roasted peanuts

- Salt to taste

- 2 cups water

- Cooked rice to serve

Directions:

1. Place a large saucepan over medium heat. Add oil. When the oil is heated, add onions and sauté until onions turn translucent.

2. Stir in garlic and ginger and sauté for a few seconds until aromatic.

3. Add Thai curry paste, sweet potatoes and peanut butter and mix well.

4. Add coconut milk and water and stir.

5. When it begins to boil, lower the heat and cook until sweet potato is fork tender. Do not cover while cooking.

6. Add spinach and salt cook for 10 minutes until sweet potatoes are very soft.

7. Turn off the heat. Add lime juice and stir.

8. Serve over cooked rice. Garnish with peanuts and serve.

Nutrition:
Calories 453,
Total Fat 23.1g
Saturated Fat 15.3g
Cholesterol 0mg
Sodium 698mg
Total Carbohydrate 55.5g

Chickpea and Squash Coconut Curry

Preparation Time: 5 Minutes
Cooking Time: 4 Minutes
Serving: 8
Ingredients:

- 2 onions, chopped

- 2 inches ginger, peeled, chopped

- 2 cloves garlic, peeled

- 2 red chilies, sliced

- 1 teaspoon turmeric powder

- 2 teaspoons ground cumin

- 2 teaspoons ground coriander

- 2 teaspoons garam masala

- 28 ounces butternut squash, peeled, diced

- 14 ounces, half Fat coconut milk

- Ounces baby spinach

- 1 tablespoon oil

- 2 cups vegetable stock or water

- Juice, lime

- Lime wedges to serve

- Salt to taste

Directions:

1. Add onion, chili, garlic and ginger into a blender. Add a tablespoon of water and blend until smooth.

2. Place a large skillet over medium heat. Add oil. When the oil is heated, add the ground paste and sauté for a few minutes until aromatic.

3. Add salt and all the spices and cook for a few seconds until aromatic.

4. Add squash and chickpeas and mix well.

5. Stir in the coconut milk and stock. When it begins to boil, lower the heat and cook until squash is soft.

6. Add spinach and cook for 3-4 minutes. Add lime juice and stir.

7. Serve over rice. Serve with lime wedges.

Nutrition:
Calories 149
Total Fat 2.5g
Saturated Fat 0.4g
Cholesterol 41mg
Sodium 68mg
Total Carbohydrate 16.5g

Chickpea Curry

Preparation Time: 5 Minutes
Cooking Time: 5 Minutes
Serving: 4
Ingredients:

- 2 tablespoons canola oil

- Salt to taste

- 1 1/2 teaspoons ground ginger

- 1 1/2 teaspoons garam masala

- 2/3 cup full Fat coconut milk

- 4 cups canned or cooked chickpeas, drained, rinsed

- 2 1/2 cups tomato puree

- A handful fresh cilantro, chopped, to garnish

Directions:

1. Place a large pot over medium-high heat. Add oil. When the oil is heated, add chickpeas, salt and the spices and mix well. Stir frequently.

2. Lower the heat to low heat. Stir in the tomato puree and coconut milk.

3. Simmer thoroughly heated. Taste and adjust the seasonings and coconut milk if required.

4. Garnish with cilantro.

5. Serve over with hot steamed rice or naan bread or any other flat bread of your choice.

Nutrition:
Calories 944
Total Fat 29g
Saturated Fat 10.3g
Cholesterol 0mg
Sodium 139mg
Total Carbohydrate 138.1g

Eggplant Mushroom and Potato Curry

Preparation Time: 5 Minutes
Cooking Time: 10 Minutes
Serving: 8
Ingredients:

- 2 tablespoons oil

- 2 pounds button mushrooms

- 2 large potatoes, peeled, chopped into chunks

- 2 eggplants, chopped into chunks

- 2 onions, chopped

- 1 1/4 cups vegetable stock

- 4 tablespoons curry paste

- 2 cans light coconut milk

- 2 tablespoons cilantro

- Salt to taste

Directions:

1. Place a large saucepan over medium heat. Add oil. When oil is heated, add onions and potatoes. Sauté for a couple of minutes. Cover and cook for about 5 minutes.

2. Add eggplants and mushrooms. Stir well. Cook for about 5 minutes.

3. Add curry paste, stock and coconut milk.

4. When it begins to boil, lower the heat and simmer until the potatoes are cooked. Garnish with cilantro and serve with hot rice or naan bread.

Nutrition:
Calories 353
Total Fat 22.8g
Saturated Fat 13.1g
Cholesterol 0mg
Sodium 52mg
Total Carbohydrate 34.5g

Tofu Cacciatore

Preparation Time: 45 minutes

Cooking Time: 35 minutes

Serving: 3

Ingredients:

- 1 14-oz. package extra firm tofu, drained

- 1 tbsp. olive oil

- 1 cup matchstick carrots

- 1 medium sweet onion, diced
- 1 medium green bell pepper, seeded, diced
- 1 28-oz. can have diced tomatoes
- 1 4-oz. can tomato paste
- ½ tbsp. balsamic vinegar
- 1 tbsp. soy sauce
- 1 tbsp. maple syrup
- 1 tbsp. garlic powder
- 1 tbsp. Italian seasoning
- ¼ tsp Salt
- ¼ tsp pepper

Directions:

1. Chop the tofu into ¼- to ½-inch cubes.

2. Warmth the olive oil in a large skillet over medium-high heat.

3. Add the onions, garlic, bell peppers, and carrots; sauté until the onions turn translucent, around 10 minutes. Make sure to stir frequently to prevent burning.

4. Now add the balsamic vinegar, soy sauce, maple syrup, garlic powder and Italian seasoning.

5. Stir well while pouring in the diced tomatoes and tomato paste; mix until all ingredients are thoroughly combined.

6. Add the cubed tofu and stir one more time.

7. Cover the pot, turn the heat to medium-low, and allow the mixture to simmer until the sauce has thickened, for around 20-25 minutes.

8. Serve the tofu cacciatore in bowls and top with salt and pepper to taste, or, store for another meal!

Nutrition:

Calories 319, Total Fat 12g, Saturated Fat 2.1g, Cholesterol 3mg, Sodium 1156mg, Total Carbohydrate 43.1g, Dietary Fiber 10.4g, Total Sugars 27.1g, Protein 17.6g, Vitamin D 0mcg, Calcium 359mg, Iron 5mg, Potassium 961mg

Muffins

Healthy Carrot Muffins

Preparation time: 10 minutes
Cooking time: 35 minutes
Servings: 2
Ingredients:

- Shredded carrots – 2 cups

- Nutmeg – 1/2 teaspoon.

- Baking powder – 1 teaspoon.

- Vanilla – 2 teaspoons.

- Ground cinnamon – 2 teaspoons.

- Maple syrup – 1/4 cup

- Coconut oil – 1/4 cup, melted

- Applesauce – 1/4 cup

- Flax meal – 1/4 cup

- Old fashioned oats – 1/4 cup

- Unsweetened almond milk – 1 cup

- Whole wheat flour – 1 1/2 cups

- Ground ginger – 1/2 teaspoon.

- Salt – 1/2 teaspoon.

Directions:

1. Preheat the oven to 350 F. Spray muffin pan with cooking spray and set aside. In a mixing bowl, mix flour, ginger, nutmeg, cinnamon, baking powder, flax meal, oats, and salt.

2. In a large bowl, whisk together almond milk, maple syrup, vanilla, coconut milk, and applesauce.

3. Add flour mixture into the almond milk mixture and mix until combined. Add shredded carrots and stir well.

4. Pour batter into the prepared muffin pan and bake for 30-35 minutes. Serve.

Nutrition:
Calories 155,
Carbs 22g,
Fat 6g,
Protein 2g

Choco Peanut Butter Muffins

Preparation time: 10 minutes
Cooking time: 20 minutes
Servings: 12
Ingredients:

- Peanut butter – 1 cup

- Baking soda – 1 teaspoon.

- Vanilla – 1 teaspoon.

- Maple syrup – 1/2 cup

- Cocoa powder – 1/2 cup

- Applesauce – 1 cup

Directions:

1. Preheat the oven to 350 F. Add all **Ingredients:** into the blender and blend until smooth.

2. Pour blended mixture into the 12 silicone muffin molds and bake for 20 minutes. Serve.

Nutrition:
Calories 175,
Carbs 17g,
Fat 11g,
Protein 6g

Easy Blueberry Muffins

Preparation time: 10 minutes
Cooking time: 25 minutes
Servings: 8
Ingredients:

- Eggs – 4

- Blueberries – 1/2 cup

- Vanilla – 1 teaspoon.

- Heavy whipping cream – 1/2 cup

- Coconut oil – 1/2 cup, melted

- Baking powder – 1 teaspoon.

- Swerve – 3 tablespoons.

- Almond flour – 2 cups

- Lemon juice – 1 tablespoon.

Directions:

1. In a large bowl, whisk eggs with lemon juice, vanilla, heavy cream, and oil. In a separate bowl, mix together almond flour, swerve, and baking powder.

2. Add almond flour mixture to the egg mixture and mix until combined. Add blueberries and fold well.

3. Pour batter in a greased muffin tray and bake at 350 F for 20-25 minutes. Serve.

Nutrition: Calories 345, Carbs 9g, Fat 32g, Protein 9g

Vanilla Banana Muffins

Preparation time: 5 minutes
Cooking time: 15 minutes
Servings: 12
Ingredients:

- Eggs – 3

- Bananas – 3, mashed

- Applesauce – 4 tablespoons.

- Honey – 1 tablespoon.

- Vanilla – 1 tablespoon.

- Baking soda – 1 teaspoon.

- Almond flour – 2 cups

- Salt – 1/2 teaspoon.

Directions:

- Preheat the oven to 350 F. Spray muffin pan with cooking spray and set aside.

- In a mixing bowl, whisk together eggs, vanilla, applesauce, honey, and bananas. In a separate bowl, mix together almond flour, baking soda, and salt.

- Add flour mixture into the egg mixture and mix well. Pour batter into the prepared muffin pan and bake for 15 minutes. Serve.

Nutrition. Calories 125, Carbs 24g, Fat 1.4, Protein 4g

Avocado and Banana Muffins

Preparation time: 20 minutes
Cooking time: 20 minutes
Servings: 12
Ingredients:

- 1/2 cup mashed avocado

- 1/2 cup mashed bananas

- 2 large eggs

- 1/2 cup milk

- 2 cups all-purpose flour

- 1 cup sugar

- 1 teaspoon baking soda

- 1 teaspoon salt

- 1/2 cup chocolate chips

Directions:

1. Preheat oven to 375 F. Grease 12 muffin tin wells or line with paper cups.

2. In a large bowl, mix avocado, bananas, eggs and milk. In a separate bowl, whisk flour, sugar, baking soda and salt. Combine with avocado mixture; do not over-mix. Stir in chocolate chips.

3. Spoon batter into prepared muffin tin; bake 15-18 minutes or until tops start to brown and a toothpick inserted into a muffin comes out clean.

Nutrition:
Calories 125,
Carbs 24g,
Fat 1.4,
Protein 4g

Avocado and Pumpkin Muffins

Preparation time: 20 minutes
Cooking time: 20 minutes
Servings: 13
Ingredients:

- 1/2 cup mashed avocado

- 11/2 cup pumpkin puree

- 2 large eggs

- 2 cups flour

- 1 cup sugar

- 1 teaspoon baking soda

- 1 teaspoon salt

- 1 teaspoon cinnamon

- 1 teaspoon vanilla

- 1/2 cup walnuts, chopped

Directions:

1. Preheat oven to 375 F. Grease 12 muffin tin wells or line with paper cups.

2. In a large bowl, mix avocado, pumpkin and eggs. In a separate bowl, whisk flour, sugar, baking soda, cinnamon, vanilla and salt.

3. Combine with avocado mixture; do not over-mix. Stir in walnuts.

4. Spoon batter into prepared muffin tin; bake 15-18 minutes or until tops start to brown and a toothpick inserted into a muffin comes out clean.

Nutrition:
Calories 225,
Carbs 14g,
Fat 1.4,
Protein 4g

Oatmeal Muffins

Preparation time: 20 minutes
Cooking time: 18 minutes
Servings: 13
Ingredients:

- 2 eggs, beaten

- 1 cup instant oatmeal

- 3/4 cup flour

- 1/2 cup sugar

- 1/2 teaspoon salt

- 2 tablespoon flaxseed

- 1 teaspoon baking powder

- 1/2 teaspoon baking soda

- 1/2 teaspoon cinnamon

- 1/3 cup walnuts, crushed

- 1/4 cup raisins

- 1/2 cup vegetable oil

- 2/3 cup milk

- 1 teaspoon lemon zest

- 1 teaspoon vanilla extract

Directions:

1. Preheat the oven to 350 F and grease 12 muffin tin wells or line with paper cups.

2. Mix together the oats, sugar, flour, salt, baking soda, baking powder, flaxseed cinnamon, walnuts and raisins.

3. In a separate bowl mix together the oil, milk, eggs, vanilla and lemon zest.

4. Pour the wet **Ingredients:** into the dry **Ingredients:** and stir for about 15 seconds, just to bring the **Ingredients:** together.

5. Scoop into the muffin tin and bake for 15 minutes or until a toothpick comes out clean. Set aside for a minute or two and transfer to a wire rack to cool completely.

Nutrition:
Calories 245,
Carbs 24g,
Fat 1.4,
Protein 4g

Conclusion

In a nutshell, this cookbook offers you a world full of options to diversify your plant-based menu. People on this diet are usually seen struggling to choose between healthy food and flavor but, soon, they run out of the options. The selection of 250 recipes in this book is enough to adorn your dinner table with flavorsome, plant-based meals every day. Give each recipe a good read and try them out in the kitchen. You will experience tempting aromas and binding flavors every day.

The book is conceptualized with the idea of offering you a comprehensive view of a plant-based diet and how it can benefit the body. You may find the shift sudden, especially if you are a die-hard fan of non-vegetarian items. But you need not give up anything that you love. Eat everything in moderation.

The next step is to start experimenting with the different recipes in this book and see which ones are your favorites. Everyone has their favorite food, and you will surely find several of yours in this book. Start with breakfast and work your way through. You will be pleasantly surprised at how tasty a vegan meal really can be.

You will love reading this book, as it helps you to understand how revolutionary a plant-based diet can be. It will help you to make informed decisions as you move toward greater change for the greater good. What are you waiting for? Have you begun your journey on the path of the plant-based diet yet? If you haven't, do it now!

Now you have everything you need to get started making budget-friendly, healthy plant-based recipes. Just follow your basic shopping list and follow your meal plan to get started! It's easy to switch over to a plant-based diet if you have your meals planned out and temptation locked away. Don't forget to clean out your kitchen before starting, and you're sure to meet all your diet and health goals.

You need to plan if you are thinking about dieting. First, you can start slowly by just eating one meal a day, which is vegetarian and gradually increasing your number of vegetarian meals. Whenever you are struggling, ask your friend or family member to support you and keep you motivated. One important thing is also to be regularly accountable for not following the diet.

If dieting seems very important to you and you need to do it right, then it is recommended that you visit a professional such as a nutritionist or dietitian to discuss your dieting plan and optimizing it for the better.

No matter how much you want to lose weight, it is not advised that you decrease your calorie intake to an unhealthy level. Losing weight does not mean that you stop eating. It is done by carefully planning meals.

A plant-based diet is very easy once you get into it. At first, you will start to face a lot of difficulties, but if you start slowly, then you can face all the barriers and achieve your goal.

Swap out one unhealthy food item each week that you know is not helping you and put in its place one of the plant-based ingredients that you like. Then have some fun creating the many different recipes in this book. Find out what recipes you like the most so you can make them often and most of all; have some fun exploring all your recipe options.

Wish you good luck with the plant-based diet!

CPSIA information can be obtained
at www.ICGtesting.com
Printed in the USA
BVHW092243260421
605885BV00002B/214